Written by **Dr. Christopher Moriarty**

Ireland

Atmosphere and impressions

TERRA SCOPE™

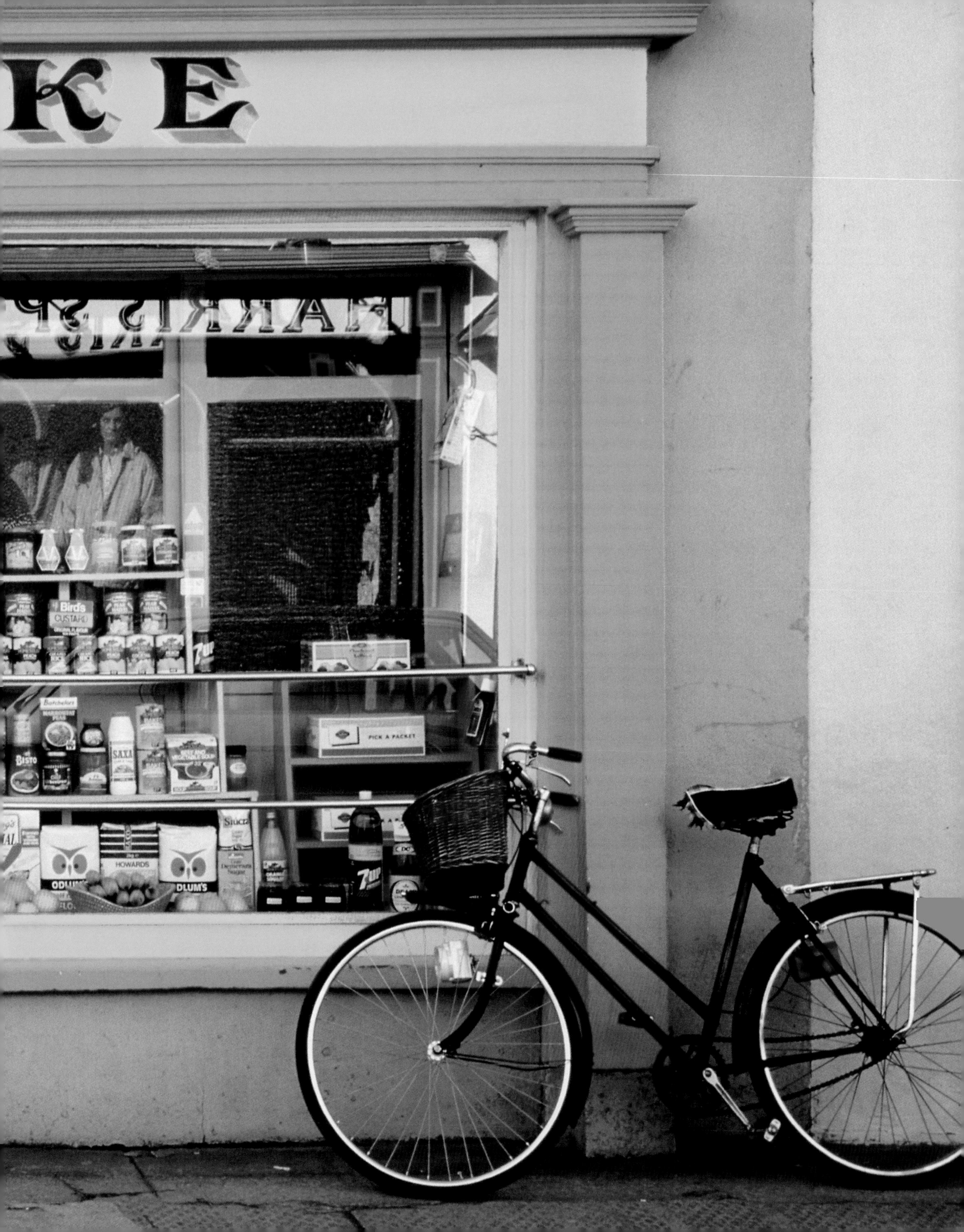
K E
Bird's
CUSTARD
PICK A PACKET
SAXA
BISTO
HOWARDS

15th century tower house in Co. Galway.

Preceeding pages:
(1) Tara Brooch – 8th century.
(2-3) Lough Corrib, "Stonewall Country", Co. Galway.
(4-5) Blasket Islands, Co. Kerry.
(6-7) Skibbereen, Co. Cork.

Publisher
In:Corporate books
Waldemar Thranesgate 77
NO-0175 Oslo
Norway

Telephone +47 22 36 06 71
Fax +47 22 20 70 39
E-mail mail@terrascope-books.com
www.terrascope-books.com

Text Christopher Moriarty
Editor Christine Aulie
Picture editor Thea Tønnessen
Translation Noricom Tolke- og Translatørtjeneste AS

Design Skomsøy Grønli as
Scanning/Pre-press Capella Media as
Printed in Aarhuus Stiftsbogtrykkerie, Denmark 2001
ISBN 82-92283-00-5

The publisher gratefully acknowledges
• Niamh Kinsella and Letitia Pollard at the Irish Tourist Board
in Dublin, for all your kind assistance and proof-reading of the book.
• Anne Langdalen and Per Erik Borge for their invaluable contributions.

Contents

Introduction

Five hundred million years ago the Iapetus Ocean was obliterated. A northwestern continent collided with one to the southeast, crumpling the rocks as if they were handwoven tweed. This is no Irish folklore or fantasy, but hard geological fact.

They were the first of a long line of disturbances which give to Ireland its endless changes of scenery and this, in turn, has been a factor in forming the character of the Irish people. One of the great joys is the impossibility of driving for more than an hour without some dramatic change in the landscape.

A hit song in the 1960s had the refrain *"Thank God we're surrounded by water"*. The boundary of Ireland is a work of nature, not of politicians. Although softened by air transport, a degree of isolation remains one of the great assets of the country. Ireland is just sufficiently remote to give visitors a feeling of achievement in getting there and the knowledge from the first landfall that they have reached a place with a very special identity.

That identity has been developing for ten thousand years, since the glaciers of the ice age receded and mesolithic hunters paddled their canoes across the sea towards the mountains they could see in the distance. The isolation was never complete and there was always two-way traffic which led from time to time to influences from outside and to Irish people travelling the world and contributing to the culture of many other nations.

→ Co. Wicklow, on the doorstep of Dublin, a region of granite mountains and lonely moorland, an escape from the busy world.

↖ ← The stone age temple of Newgrange built and embellished with abstract sculpture, 5,000 years ago, to face the rising sun at midwinter.

↑ Portrait of Christ from the Gospel manuscript, the Book of Kells. Written and illuminated by monks in the 8th century, it may be seen at Trinity College, Dublin.

But, back on the island, the people developed things in their own, special, way. Before the Egyptians built the pyramids, a neolithic community created the great temple complex of Newgrange. While much of Europe suffered disruption in the dark ages, Ireland remained relatively peaceful and was a haven of Christian thought and practice - with a wonderful flowering of painting and sculpture, culminating in the magnificent Book of Kells and the great stone Celtic crosses.

A bit of chance, a bit of charm, and a great deal of brainpower led, in the closing years of the 20th century, to the emergence of the Celtic Tiger. Ireland, quite suddenly, became an affluent country. Explosive growth of high-tech industries including financial services, computers and chemicals has been accompanied by a new degree of pressure for the care of the country-side and the best things of the old way of life. The Ireland of the 21st century remains a land where there is space and time. The space is there for those who want, for a while, to "get away from it all", the time for people, native and visitor, to relax and talk or just to contemplate. This book aims to preserve on paper a little of that atmosphere.

History

The distant past

According to ancient monastic annals, the first people of Ireland landed in 2680 BC. Archaeologists do better, with evidence of mesolithic hunter-gatherers from 8000 BC or earlier. They made a range of implements from the flint which is plentiful in the magnificent chalk cliffs of County Antrim. A profound change – and one which would dominate Irish life into the 19th century and beyond – took place about five thousand years ago. Agriculture was introduced by neo-lithic people who developed a high civilisation.

↘ This 8th century ministerial chalice is an exquisite example of the craft of the Irish early Christian metalworkers and is probably the most famous object in the National Museum.

Metalwork first appeared about 2000 BC and the museums have rich collections celebrating the achievements of the Bronze Age people. Some of it is utilitarian: knives, axes and cauldrons. But there was gold in the river gravel and goldsmiths created exquisite jewellery and ornaments.

The final period of pre-history was the Iron Age, coincidental with the introduction of a Celtic language, and dated to about 600 BC. Traces of thousands of dwellings of this time remain, among them colossal stone buildings such as Staigue Fort in Kerry and Dun Aengus on the Aran Islands. The activities of these people's kings, heroes and druids are familiar to us through legend and saga.

↑ Staigue Fort, Co. Kerry. The best preserved Iron Age fort in Ireland.

↑↑ A memorial stone on the Dingle peninsula, bearing an inscription in the pre-Christian Ogham alphabet.

← 16th century Dunluce Castle, Co. Antrim where the cliff once gave away, taking the kitchen with it and seriously disrupting a banquet.

↑ Clonmacnoise, Co. Offaly, one of the greatest
of the ancient monasteries.
*"In a quiet watered land, a land of roses,
stands Saint Kieran's city fair
And the warriors of Ireland
in their thousands slumber there..."* T.W.Rolleston.

↑↑ White Island, early Christian sculpture,
Co. Fermanagh.

← St Macdara's Island church, Co. Galway.

The early Christians

In AD 432 St Patrick's vision led him
to visit the small groups of Christians
who lived in Ireland. Within his
lifetime, Christianity had completely
assimilated and replaced the existing
druidic religion. In the course of the
next few centuries, Christian monks,
scholars and artists introduced writing
and developed calligraphy, metalwork
and sculpture to a degree never to be
surpassed.

They re-introduced building in stone
and much remains of their work.
The great monasteries., Clonmacnoise
and Glendalough, among many
others, were colleges which attracted
the sons of the wealthy from all parts
of Ireland and far beyond. Meanwhile,
a host of missionaries, Columba,
Columbanus and Killian among
others, spread their particular form
of Christianity as far afield as Italy and
Germany.

For seven hundred years the Celtic church remained to some degree aloof from Rome but, in the 12th century, Irish church leaders introduced reformed rites and established a firm connection with the Papacy. This included invitations to the Cistercians and other continental monastic orders. Beginning at Mellifont, they introduced both Gothic architecture and major agricultural reforms.

↑ Glendalough, Co. Wicklow, 11th century
buildings of the monastery founded by St. Kevin
five hundred years earlier.

↖ Mellifont, Co. Louth, 12th century monastery.

← Boa Island Iron Age idol, Co. Fermanagh.

The Vikings

For some centuries, all was peaceful: people killed and pillaged their friends and relations to an acceptable degree or indulged in raiding expeditions across the Irish Sea. Then, from 795, Vikings arrived, using safe anchorages around the coast as strategic bases for raiding. Sometimes unsupported, but often with the help of native Irish war lords, they introduced new weapons and techniques and earned a very bad reputation. Whether their incursions had a lasting effect on monastic life, beyond the horrors of scattered massacres and burnings, is uncertain. During the two centuries or more of these attacks, monastic art, literature, philosophy and building continued unabated, leading to some of their greatest achievements, including the round towers and the Celtic crosses.

The Vikings made a notable contribution to Irish life in establishing the seaports which developed into the principal cities. At first worshipping the Nordic gods, they adopted Christianity and established themselves as an integral part of society. Simplistic history books relate how the great Irish king Brian Boru expelled the Danes at the Battle of Clontarf in 1014 – but in fact there were Nordic and Irish people on both sides and many of the former continued to live in peace.

The Anglo-Normans

The 12th century witnessed the most profound political revolution known to Irish history. The King of Leinster, Dermot Mac Murrough, enlisted the aid of a warrior from Wales, the Anglo-Norman nicknamed "Strongbow", in a personal battle with the O'Connor kings of Connaught.

An agreement between King Henry II and Pope Adrian IV in 1155 had led to the king of England regarding himself as legitimate sovereign of Ireland and, in 1169, the first substantial contingent of Anglo-Normans landed on Bannow Island on the southeast coast. This was the beginning of more than seven hundred years of English rule.

Although Anglo-Norman warlords seized most of the good agricultural land, rule from the neighbouring island was far from complete. Evidence of the feeling of insecurity of the invaders remains in the great castle of Trim and many hundreds of lesser ones. Many of the Gaelic kings survived and ruled their territories, while before long the invaders became "more Irish than the Irish themselves". Until the 17th century, much of the Gaelic way of life, including religion, poetry and music, prospered under hereditary patrons old and new.

The final invasions

While England became Protestant, Ireland remained largely Catholic. Beginning with Queen Mary in 1556, a succession of English monarchs seized large areas of good land and colonised them with their supporters from England and Scotland. In contrast to the previous invasions and infiltrations, the early 17th century Protestant settlers of the Plantation in Ulster were not to be assimilated into the old community.

↑ Rock of Dunamase, Co. Laois.

→ Tall Cross at Monasterboice, Co. Louth, one of the 9th century stone "scripture crosses" set up in the Celtic monasteries and adopted as an emblem of Ireland.

Not surprisingly, the original owners of the land struggled to retain it. Warfare over more than a century led to a virtual cessation of cultural development and spelled the end of the traditional Gaelic aristocracy. The 1607 Flight of the Earls, when the last great chieftains O'Donnell and O'Neill left Ireland for exile in Europe, completed the transfer to rule from England.

Twice in the 17th century, Ireland backed the wrong side in English conflicts. In the Cromwellian civil war, a majority of Irish took the Royalist side and, not long afterwards, many of the survivors supported the Jacobites and lost to King William in the epic battles of the Boyne and Aughrim.

Savage Penal Laws were then drawn up to suppress Catholics and other Christians outside the Anglican Church. Their victims, the great majority of the people, were effectively barred from the professions, from land-ownership and from freely practising their religion.

← ↖ Bunratty Castle, Co. Clare, built in the 14th century, restored in the 20th and offering "medieval banquets" to show how things used to be.

← 15th century Ross Castle, Killarney.

↑ Clifden - capital of Connemara, Co. Galway.

↗ Dublin's Custom House, designed by James
Gandon, the architect responsible for many
of the best 18th century public buildings
of the capital.

→→ Bank of Ireland, Dublin originally built
in 1730 as the Parliament House.

→ Castletown House, Co. Kildare - the greatest
of the 18th century mansions.

Dublin became a great parliamentary capital, a European rather than a provincial city. Splendid public buildings, town houses arranged around open greens and a busy harbour were built. The 16th century University of Dublin, together with many hospitals and public institutions were supported by government funds and by wealthy individuals.

Parliament and 1798

As the 18th century advanced, the descendants of the colonists, together with those of the older landowners who, one way or another, had retained their family property, began to feel secure. Ireland was ruled by its own parliament – exclusively Protestant and therefore unrepresentative but nonetheless deeply concerned with the betterment of the people. Great estates, with beautiful classical residences were created and new churches and villages built beside them. The Irish countryside took on much of the shape it has retained to this day.

Beneath the surface republican ideals were developing, inspired by revolution in America and France. Armed insurrection in 1798 was quickly defeated by the authorities. But it sowed the seeds of nationalism and a desire for fully representative government with equal rights for "Protestant, Catholic and Dissenter" as Wolfe Tone, the inspirational leader of the movement, put it.

↑ Memorial at City Quay, Dublin, to the millions who died or emigrated at the time of the great famine 1847-1849.

The century of the Famine

The rising of 1798 was followed by the Act of Union of 1800 amalgamating the British and Irish parliaments. One of the most impressive of all Irish leaders emerged soon afterwards. Daniel O'Connell, a Catholic landowner, conducted the campaign for religious freedom, which was attained in 1829. This peaceful revolution led to a great wave of church building and profound social change.

Meanwhile, the population increased rapidly, reaching the 8 million mark by the early 1840s, the great majority being subsistence farmers living on the western seaboard. In 1845, the potato, their staple diet, began to succumb to fungal disease and famine reached an appalling height in 1847. In spite of great efforts towards relief inappropriate government ideology, combined with a measure of incompetence, allowed more than a million to die. A further three million would leave the stricken country for America, beginning a pattern of emigration which would persist for more than a hundred years.

The latter years of the 19th century saw the rise of the romantic parliamentary leader Charles Stewart Parnell and a wave of improvement in agriculture and industry. Revolution this time was peaceful, leading to the ownership of land by the peasants. The same period saw a revival of interest in the Irish language and in all forms of traditional culture.

Towards the 21st century

In the first decade of the 20th century art, education, theatre and literature – to say nothing of agriculture, fisheries and forestry - entered a dramatic era of innovation and growth. At the same time nationalist politics surged ahead. The brief insurrection of Easter 1916 ended tragically but sparked off the final move towards independence. The early 1920s saw the division of Ireland into the Free State of 26 counties governed from Dublin and the 6 north-eastern counties as Northern Ireland, a province of the UK administered by a parliament in Belfast. In 1949 the Free State became the fully independent Republic of Ireland. Self-government of the six counties of Northern Ireland was abolished in 1972 but an Assembly, established in 1999, restored a measure of democratic control.

The 1950s saw the beginning of the change from a rural to an industrial economy and the end of the downward trend in population. Generous tax incentives led international firms to set up factories in Ireland. There were ups and downs, and progress in Northern Ireland was severely affected by political violence. But the overall trend was towards a brighter, better fed, better educated and healthier Ireland. Accession to the European Union in 1973 resulted in generous support for agriculture and the infrastructure in general. These factors led in the 1990s to the upward surge in the economy, the "Celtic Tiger".

City Life

Dublin

The Irish words "Dubh Linn" translate as "a dark pool" and that was where the Vikings found a safe anchorage in the 9th century. Their town provided archaeologists with a marvellous collection of artefacts which makes one of the finest exhibits in the National Museum. The High Street of the Vikings retains its name and Christchurch Cathedral looks down over the river from the site of their first church.

When the Anglo-Normans came, they built a castle near Christchurch. Later, St Patrick's Cathedral was built outside the city walls and Trinity College was established on the site of an old monastery nearby. The castle and cathedrals have survived from medieval times but little else remains visible of ancient Dublin. It took the inspiration of a number of 18th century landowners and clergy to create the beautiful city that is the centre of things today. They were responsible for the splendid public buildings: Trinity College, the Parliament House (now the Bank of Ireland), the law courts and the Custom House.

← Trinity College, Dublin: 18th and 19th century buildings.

Following page: The Long Room, Trinity College Library, - a busy working library in an 18th century home with a fabulous collection of manuscripts ancient and modern.

With a population of more than one million, modern Dublin is a busy and dynamic city. Parliament meets in Leinster House, a classical mansion built by the Duke of Leinster in 1745. For more than a hundred years before Independence, it was the headquarters of the Royal Dublin Society which developed the national library, museums and art gallery. These institutions remain in place making the site, together with Trinity College just down the road, a compact centre displaying five thousand years of Irish art and learning.

The legendary Abbey Theatre, focus of the great literary revival at the turn of the 19th century, is across the river – as is the Municipal Gallery of Modern Art. Shopping and cafés straddle the Liffey, as do the pubs. Dublin's most recent developments are Temple Bar and Smithfield.

Temple Bar, a riverside conglomeration of 18th and 19th century dwellings, is now the hub of eating, drinking, singing, performing and, in a dazzling variety of galleries, exhibiting the most exciting work of contemporary artists. At Smithfield, a great area of cobbled market space has been transformed to a fashionable, tree-shaded square, centred on a viewing tower made from the great chimney of the former Jameson distillery. Dublin has never been so vibrant with life.

← Four Courts and River Liffey, Dublin.

↓ St. Patrick's Cathedral, Dublin, founded in 1191.

↓↓ Adam and Eve's Church, Dublin.

↓ The "Pepperpot" Church, Mount Street, Dublin.

← ↓ Temple Bar in the centre of Dublin,
riverside assemblage of art galleries, sculpture,
good food, fabulous pubs, song and dance
and a weekend food-market.

← Reginald's Tower, Waterford.

↗ St. Colman's Cathedral, Cobh, Co. Cork.

→ St. Finn Barr's Cathedral, Cork.

Waterford

A stark circular tower stands near the quayside at Waterford. Founded by Reginald the Dane in 1003, it was rebuilt in the 12th century and beautifully restored in the 20th. A safe anchorage, sheltered by hills and providing, through its three rivers, access to much of the richest land in the country, Waterford has been a top seaport for a thousand years.

Industry developed in the 18th century. The most renowned product is the exquisite lead crystal glass. A former granary now houses a superb new museum, presenting Viking jewellery, the 14th century Charter and a host of other treasures of the old city.

Cork

Cork grew up on the slopes of the deep valley of the River Lee. Its population of 150,000 places makes it the first city of the south. The 19th century cathedral stands where St. Finn Barr founded a monastery in the 6th century and the city began. Besides a small number of 18th century town houses and St. Anne's Church at Shandon, with its legendary peal of bells, the greater part of Cork dates from the 19th century. The beautiful campus of the university was begun in 1845.

Cork claims the only opera house in Ireland and the principal school of ballet. The streets and houses climbing the hillsides give it a special atmosphere, something the citizens cherish and are more than willing to share with their visitors. Perhaps that is why Cork has a special place in the hearts of those who organise or go to festivals. Cork International Film Festival and its Jazz Festival are some of the most exciting gatherings that Ireland can offer.

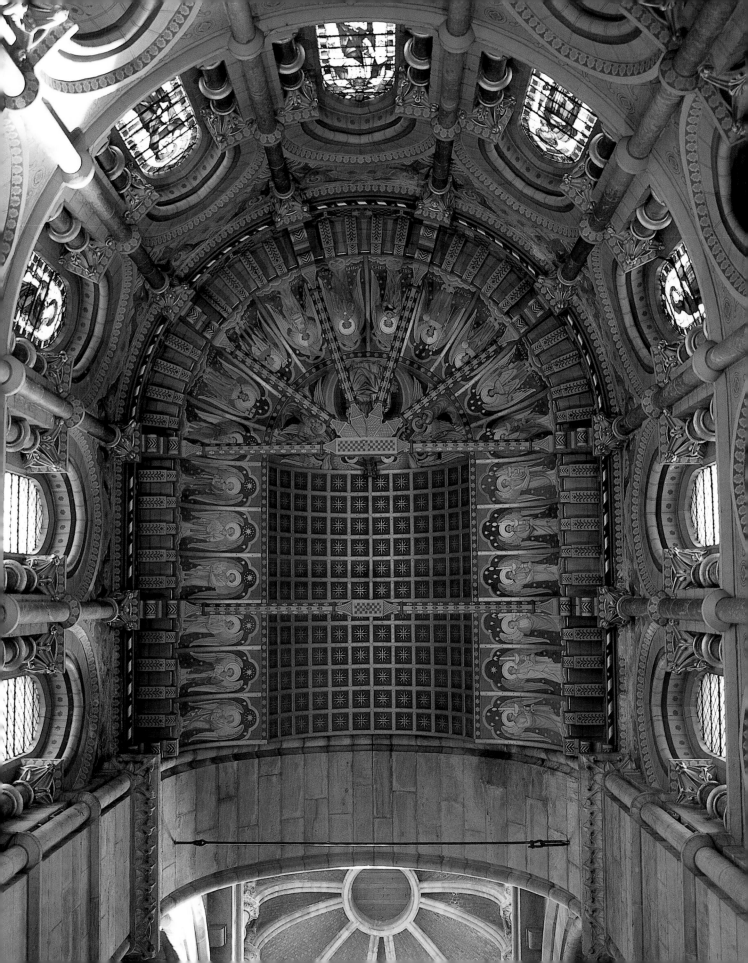

Limerick

The first crossing point on the lordly River Shannon, had to be a place of the greatest strategic significance and it was here the Vikings created a seaport. The great castle built by the English King John in 1210 still stands and is the centre of a delightfully restored ancient waterfront. A treaty signed in 1691 led to peace and prosperity and the legacy of beautiful 18th century houses. Limerick entered the 21st century following the opening of a new university and the superb Hunt Museum and an influx of young people to man the expanding hi-tech industries.

Galway

Where it enters Galway Bay, the River Corrib divides into many channels. Here in the 13th century, the town of Galway began to become a flourishing seaport, trading directly with Spain and other continental countries. Even older traditions survived outside the city in the Claddagh.

The building of the University, close to the river bank in 1849, was one of the key factors in re-establishing Galway as a place of consequence. The Irish-language Taibhdhearc Theatre has flourished for fifty years, while the much younger Druid Theatre has become a byword for the best in drama. Thanks largely to the computer industry, the last two decades of the 20th century have seen a transformation from quaint and old-fashioned to modern and bustling. The great Galway celebrations are centred on arts, oysters and horses – but a festival atmosphere is a permanent feature of the capital of the West.

Kilkenny

Kilkenny's life as a major city began in 1170 when the Anglo-Norman warlord Strongbow built a clifftop castle overlooking the River Nore. A little way to the north, a cathedral was built and between the two a town grew up, rivalling Dublin in importance. To this day, Kilkenny retains a delightful medieval atmosphere.

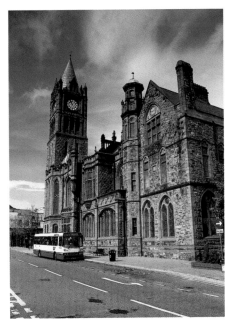

← The Spanish Arch, Galway.

↑ Galway - neither the Celtic Tiger nor an influx of hi-tech industry could conquer the relaxed, Bohemian atmosphere of the city.

↗ Derry's Guild Hall.

↙ Kilkenny Castle – fortress, family home, now a centre for arts and crafts.

With its gardens and art gallery, the castle is now one of the great showpieces of modern Ireland. Across the road, the opulent stables have been rebuilt to house the Kilkenny Design Centre, with its shopping emporium offering the absolute best in Irish clothing and craftwork.

Derry

St Columba founded a monastery in 546 on a hillside overlooking broad and beautiful Lough Foyle. In the course of the next thousand years it became a cathedral town and seaport. Everything changed in 1613 when a consortium of London merchants invested in the development of the city. They had formidable walls built to protect the community of Protestant settlers within, and renamed it Londonderry.

Within the walls, Derry retains more traces of 17th century life than any other Irish city. The 19th century saw prosperity and the creation of splendid Victorian neo-gothic buildings, foremost amongst them the Guildhall with its brilliant stained-glass windows. Derry in recent years has been a model of co-operation between Nationalist and Unionist and is a most delightful place to visit.

Belfast

The origins of the modern city can be traced to 1603 when Sir Arthur Chichester began to develop a town which rapidly became the major seaport of the northeast. Towards the end of the 18th century the linen industry developed. Later, the ship-yards of Belfast came to be numbered amongst the world's greatest, the birthplace not only of the "Titanic" but of many of the finest ocean liners ever built. The giant cranes of Harland and Wolff still dominate the skyline.

A child of the Industrial Revolution of the early 19th century, Belfast reflects Victorian and Edwardian opulence in its flamboyant and lavishly decorated buildings. It became a great cultural centre with Botanic Gardens established in 1839 and proudly displaying one of the earliest and most beautiful tropical glass houses. The Queen's University, still an integral part of city life, was founded in 1849. The City Hall, completed in 1906, was conceived as the central point of a city which, at the time, almost equalled Dublin in size and surpassed the capital in wealth.

Modern Belfast, with a population of half a million is a thrilling city. It is now almost free from more than a music flourish. The centre is largely a reserve for pedestrians with a multitude of shops and restaurants. The Ulster Museum houses the treasures of the Spanish Armada galeass "Girona", sunk on the north coast in 1588. The magnificent Waterfront Hall, built in the 1990s, shows Belfast's new sense of confidence in a peaceful and prosperous future.

↑ Waterfront Hall, Belfast.

↗ Belfast City Hall, the opulent administrative headquarters of the second city of Ireland.

Nature

The seaside

Augustine, a 7th century Irish monk, made the discovery that our country had once been connected by land to the neighbouring landmass. But that connection disappeared a long time ago. Countless thousands of years of buffeting have given the coast of Ireland its infinite variety of stupendous cliffs, idyllic strands and wild estuaries.

Railways in the 19th century made bathing places available to holiday makers and a brave new world began of hotels, gracious terraced houses and yacht clubs. The 20th century saw a great upsurge of water sports and an explosion of golf links on the sand dunes.

← ↗ The Cliffs of Moher, Co. Clare.

The Cliffs of Moher make a bid to offer the most spectacular coastal scenery: miles of sheer rock dropping 200 metres to the ocean. Slieve League is the highest cliff, steep enough to be terrifying but with just enough slope to allow wild flowers to grow in abundance and for a road to take you close to the summit.
Or you may seek the marvellous black basalt of the Giant's Causeway and the dazzling white chalk of Whitepark Bay.

↑ → The Giant's Causeway, Co. Antrim; geologists ascribe it to a volcanic eruption 60 million years ago, but everybody knows it was built by a giant who wanted to reach Scotland without getting his feet wet.

↑ Cumeenoole Beach on the Kerry Coast.

→ The three Aran Islands preserve the Irish language and many traditional ways of life: cars are few and footpaths plentiful.

Rocky coasts have their own special attractions, particularly in early summer when pink, yellow and white wild flowers make a garden of the coastal roadsides. In winter the estuaries are busy with thousands of wild geese, duck and wading birds. Seals and dolphins hunt in sight of the shore and there are a few special dolphin-watching points such as Kilrush in the Shannon Estuary.

The popular seaside places depend in the first place on the strand: mile after mile of sand and sand dune and water that is free from pollution. Resorts such as Tramore, Rossnowlagh and Inch offer a conglomeration of seaside entertainments and crowded swimming places at the near end of the strand. Elsewhere, hidden coves and more huge strands offer space and tranquility. We have a lot of space in Ireland.

The islands
Achill is the biggest island, the Arans the most romantic, Skellig Michael the most dramatic and Tory the most menacing – at least in legend.
The Blaskets are the most fertile ground for literature and Clare Island is the most meticulously studied.
But every one of the hundreds of islands around the coast of Ireland has its own superlative.

↑ The 7th century monastery of Skellig Michael,
on a remote rock pinnacle off the coast of Kerry.

→ The Blasket Islands, Co. Kerry.

→→ Tory Island, Co. Donegal.

Achill offers high mountains and cliffs, the finest strand on any island and good accommodation. The Aran Islands, all three of them, have a thriving population of Irish-speaking farmers and fishermen. They became known throughout the world through the writings of J. M. Synge and from Robert Flaherty's 1934 film "Man of Aran".

Skellig Michael, a steep, remote and barren rock stack seven miles out in the Atlantic, was the home for centuries of a community of monks whose stone-built dwellings cluster over the higher parts and have withstood the weather for more than a thousand years. Close by is the Little

Skellig, inhabited by a colony of thousands of gannets, gigantic white seabirds.

Tory, on the north coast, was the home of the evil giant Balor in mythological times. It earned particular fame in the 20th century from the paintings of the fisherman James Dixon. Two great works were written in the Irish language by the Blasket islanders Tomás Ó Criomthainn and Maurice O'Sullivan.

And that's only a selection!

↑ Great Sugarloaf, Co. Wicklow.

The mountains

*"While I long for the dear one
that's waiting for me
Where the Mountains of Mourne
sweep down to the sea"*

So sang the popular composer Percy French, endowing that particularly fine range with immortality. In common with all the mountains of Ireland, the Mournes are mere hillocks by world standards. The highest peak in the country, Carrantuohill in the McGillicuddy's Reeks of County Kerry is the only one to top 1,000 metres.

Most of the mountains have gentle slopes and rounded tops. But there are some specials. The Great Sugarloaf in county Wicklow is small but steep and stands out on its own from the main range, thereby giving a fantastic view. Ben Bulben forms a great wall of rock rising suddenly to tower above the lowlands and Croagh Patrick has been a place of pilgrimage since pagan times.

And there are little specialities. The stone-age farmers liked to make mountain-top tombs for their distinguished dead. Glaciers created wonderful deep corrie lakes, tucked in to the hillside at the bottom of steep cliffs. Beautiful little Alpine flowers, saxifrages in particular, bloom amongst the rocks.

What constitutes a mountain in Ireland is its unsuitability for people to live on its slopes. A combination of high rainfall and poor, peaty soil puts the higher slopes far outside the possibilities of profitable agriculture. So nobody lives there and, most important, there are few field boundaries and hill-walkers are free to wander over the heather.

← Tim Healy Pass, Co. Kerry.

51

Rivers and lakes

Rivers meant so much to the people of ancient Ireland that some of the greatest of them, Shannon, Boyne and Liffey, still bear the names that were given to them in a forgotten language thousands of years ago. Besides life-giving water they provided the ancients with abundant fish and wildfowl – as they still do for modern visitors.

↖ Macgillycuddy's Reeks, Co. Kerry
– Ireland's highest mountains.

←← *"Under bare Ben Bulben's head, in Drumcliffe churchyard Yeats is laid."*
The dramatic limestone escarpment in County Sligo captivated Ireland's greatest poet.

The Shannon, with its tributaries, covers one third of the country. Rising from a mystical spring on a remote mountainside, it flows for 199 miles to meet the tide at Limerick. On its journey it widens in places to form some of the most beautiful lakes in the land: Ree of the wide lowlands, Allen and Derg surrounded by mountains - and many others.

Weirs and canals built in the 18th century opened the Shannon to shipping. Today thousands of pleasure boats explore hundreds of miles of peaceful waterway. In the 1990s old canals were reopened to connect the Shannon to her neighbour the Erne to add yet more lakes and rivers to this wonderland.

Lough Neagh is the biggest of the Irish lakes, 150 square miles of open water. Its population of eels provides a livelihood for four hundred fishermen. The lakes of Killarney, cradled amongst misty mountains, are deservedly renowned for the haunting beauty of their scenery. Another Lough Derg, hidden away amongst barren moorland, has been a place of Christian pilgrimage since the dark ages. The River Boyne flows around the earthly palace of Aengus, the god of love. Away in the west the great lakes of Corrib, Mask and Carra separate the fertile lands to the east from the magnificent mountains and moorland of Connemara.

In literature, W. B. Yeats described the beauties of Lough Gill in his poem "The Lake Isle of Innisfree". James Joyce, fascinated by the river's almost circular journey of 75 miles , made the River Liffey the heroine of his bewildering novel "Finnegan's Wake". The Elizabethan poet Edmund Spencer wrote romantic tales of the lives and loves of the rivers. And the ancient Irish deified, personified and glorified the waters great and small.

↑ Lough Mask, Co. Mayo.

→ Upper Lake, Killarney, Co. Kerry.

↑ → Traditionally cut peat in Connemara, Co. Galway.

The peatlands

Climate changes eight or nine thousand years ago endowed about one fifth of the land of Ireland with a covering of peat bog. Most of it was spread over areas of lowland in the arms of the River Shannon. Closer to the Atlantic Ocean, in the west of Ireland following a period of high

rainfall and also on mountains throughout the land, a blanket of peat grew up and covered hill and valley.

The peat forms an acid soil, drains badly and is generally inhospitable to man or beast. Nonetheless, it is bright with wild flowers and in places covered with woodland. Soft, wet and unproductive, the bog was something of a no-man's land – except for the fact that the lowlands never go on for too long. Ridges and isolated hills criss cross the peat and these provide good land. So there have been countless generations of thriving communities on the edge of the bog. They used the peat for fuel, buried butter for storage and now and again buried their most precious treasures. Some of these now grace museum collections and archaeologists have laid bare trackways and field divisions made by the people who farmed before the peat grew up.

Since the 1950s, great quantities of peat have been excavated by colossal yellow-painted machines which travel slowly across the surface. It is used to generate electricity, as an non-polluting domestic fuel and as a garden soil conditioner. The "cutaway" from these undertakings is transformed to forest, grassland, even to new lakelands and wildlife reserves. At the same time, huge tracts of untouched bog have been taken over by conservation authorities to ensure that examples of this unique and beautiful landscape can be preserved.

↑ Mullaghmore Burren landscape, Co. Clare.

← Mechanically extracted peat.

The Burren

Picture a landscape that is grey instead of green, rising to high mountains and pounded by the waves of the Atlantic. That is the broad view of the Burren. The close-up reveals that even the grey comes in different shades, that it is punctuated by little patches of green pasture and bright with the yellows, whites and purples of a host of wild flowers, which grow in the innumerable cracks and fissures of the rock.

May is its brightest month, with spring flowers in full bloom. They are more than simply beautiful. For example, the white-flowered dryas is one of the most abundant. It is also common in arctic Norway and the Swiss Alps, anywhere closer it is an extreme rarity. The blue gentian, another Alpine flower, is one of the most exquisite of the Burren garden and there are many rare saxifrages. Growing in the same region are species such as the maidenhair fern whose normal home is the Mediterranean. It is far from fully understood how these outlandish plants can flourish in this small part of Ireland.

The Burren would be worth it just for the flowers – and there are more and more of them through the summer. But it was also a thriving community of stone-age farmers and the region is liberally scattered with their monuments: dolmens, gallery graves and others constructed from huge slabs of limestone. Archaeologists have surveyed and excavated them, artists and postcard makers reproduced them – but nobody has penetrated their mystery.

Only one river flows above the ground in the Burren. But beneath the surface lies a labyrinth of caverns, one at Ailwee made safe and welcoming for all visitors. Others have been charted and are well known to experts, yet others remain unknown – measureless to man. The Burren is a region of sheer magic.

Culture

The people

Julius Caesar wrote of the welcome given by the Celtic tribes - the Gauls - to people from foreign lands. Whatever its origin, the image of Irish people remains as hospitable, full of talk - but willing to listen - and with all the time in the world to engage in these activities. Strong evidence that this is more than a cosy myth lies in the success of the tourist industry in a country where sunny weather can never be taken for granted - but, more importantly, where it never rains in the pub.

Few truly historical figures appeared until the arrival in the 5th century of Ireland's patron Saint Patrick. Like many after him, Patrick was an immigrant who became fully identified with his people and country. Columba, a century later, combined a warlord's temperament with religious fervour and flourished as a preacher and diplomat in Scotland.

Archetypal saints, heroes and kings illustrate characteristics admired throughout the ages. While the lethal battles of old have been replaced by team games and politics, poets, musicians and writers continue to be honoured. Like the Christian religion, settlers, even armed ones, became fully absorbed and the Celtic ancestry has been leavened by the assimilation of people of many races.

Festivals

St. Patrick's Day, celebrated the world over wherever there are people of Irish descent, is the great national holiday. The centre of Dublin and many other towns are taken over by parades of industry and culture with street theatre, fireworks and a good time for all. Horse racing, football, hurling and all the associated vigorous sports enjoy a day of frenzied activity, while the spectators wrap up well against the cold March wind. Shamrock, the three-leaved clover said to have been used by the saint to explain the Trinity, is worn as a badge by one and all.

← Ireland is a land of music – brass bands, pipe bands, choirs, traditional singers, pop groups and symphony orchestras: some make money, others work hard for support.

↑ St. Patrick's Day Parade, 17th March – passing
12th century Christchurch, Dublin's oldest
cathedral.

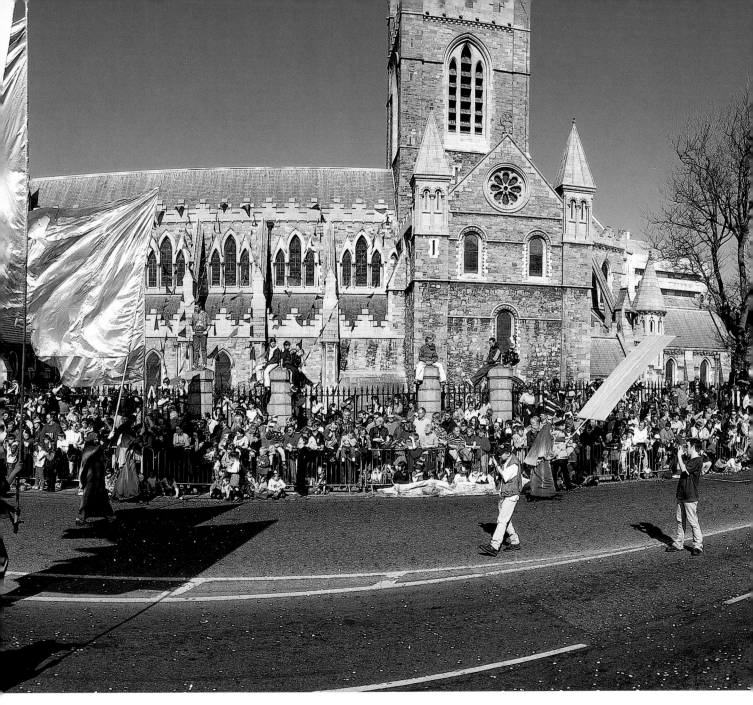

↑ → Horses are reared, owned and ridden by rich and poor all over Ireland. The Ballinasloe Horse Fair in Co. Galway brings all sorts together every October.

The Irish language

Together with Scots, Irish belongs to one of the two surviving branches of Celtic languages and probably became established in its older form about 2,500 years ago. Irish continued to be the language of the majority of the people and of the Gaelic aristocracy through the first four centuries following the Anglo-Norman invasion.

It was still the language of scholars in the 17th century when the Franciscan monk Michael O'Clery and three colleagues compiled the "Annals of the Four Masters". But its fortunes declined, especially since the language of state education in the 19th century was English.

There are, of course, church services on the patron saint's day. But other holy days are more intensely religious, the greatest being the annual pilgrimage to the summit of Croagh Patrick, attended by thousands from all parts of Ireland on the last Sunday in July.

There are annual festivals for film in Cork, theatre in Dublin and amateur drama in Athlone, to say nothing of the Fleadh Ceoil where traditional musicians gather, perform and drink in a different town every year.
Then there are the summer schools where you may learn about Ireland, about Yeats or about music and midwinter gatherings such as the mummer's festival in Woodford on the edge of the Slieve Aughty Mountains. Festivals are fun, frequent and increasing in numbers and variety every year.

At the same time, however, academics had begun intensive work to preserve Irish writings and a popular revival of interest began towards the end of the 19th century. Independence was to see the introduction of the Irish language to all school curricula and the 1937 Constitution designated it the "first official language". Most Irish people are not enthusiastic about official views and continue to speak, write and sing in English.

← The 19th century Pro-Cathedral in Dublin.

Although dramatic progress has been made in Northern Ireland towards reconciliation between Protestant and Catholic, much sectarian bitterness remains. Religious tolerance of the 3% of Protestants and others in the Republic has usually been the rule and ecumenical ideas have been adopted with enthusiasm.

Religion

For the first seven centuries, Irish Christianity was centred on some hundreds of monasteries, ranging in size from anchorite's cells to university cities with thousands of students. A twelfth century reform altered the system to one of dioceses with three archbishops in command.

The Reformation and its adoption by King Henry VIII saw the beginning of two centuries of catastrophic change, accompanied by warfare: first the dissolution of the monasteries and then concerted efforts to make Ireland Protestant. The establishment of the Anglican Church as the religion of the rulers led to the Catholic faith of the majority being subservient until as recently as 1869.

↑ On the last Sunday in July, thousands of pilgrims climb the rocky track to the summit of Croagh Patrick, Co. Mayo where St. Patrick fasted for 40 days.

↓ Sheep pasture in the Wicklow Mountains.

Farming

When the first farmers came, about five thousand years ago, the greater part of Ireland was covered in oak forest. It was cleared so slowly that Ireland remained a well-wooded land. All changed in the 17th century when new settlers felled the trees and sold the timber.

The 18th century witnessed renewed interest in forestry and subsidies offered to develop woodland. At the same time, the system of grazing changed and the formerly open fields came to be enclosed within hedges, creating the familiar landscape pattern of large and small fields.

A combination of mild climate with the rich limestone soil of the midlands, allowed cattle to live in the open throughout the year, their feed being supplemented first by hay, later by silage. Cattle were the mainstay of Irish agriculture, yielding superb meat and abundant dairy products. Recent years have seen the development of a marvellous variety of farm-produced cheeses. Intensive raising of chickens and livestock has grown apace. But the image of Ireland as a land, where sheep and cattle graze peacefully on green pasture, remains a true one and the countryside seems set to continue in its old, delightfully unkempt, ways.

Food and drink

Beef and salmon were so plentiful and so very good that, until the 18th century, the people of Ireland were extremely well fed. Add to these pork, lamb, chicken, ducks and geese and, of course, potatoes, and you may have an explanation of our failure to develop a tradition for frogs, snails and similar small creatures.

A transformation of Irish eating habits took place in the second half of the 20th century. All the cities and larger towns today offer a mouthwatering variety of restaurants at all price ranges. Even more exciting are the villages, such as Schull on the south coast, which have become famous for the number and quality of their eating houses. Meanwhile, farmhouse cheeses and an incredible variety of seafood have been added to an already excellent menu.

Once the preserve of the Irish male, the pub has come to welcome all sorts and conditions of men and women. It remains the centre of the community where conversation ranges from high politics to low gossip, from dissection of the current ball game to learned observations on the weather – all lubricated with a pint of stout or a glass of whiskey or even a mineral water – and accompanied in many cases by live and lively music and sometimes by dancing. Local and stranger, peasant and city sophisticate – all are overcome by the warmth and hospitality of this unique institution.

↓ Arthur Guinness brewed his first dark ale in 18th century Dublin and created a way of life for the world.

← ↙ Irish whiskey, after distillation, spends years
maturing in wine barrels.

Music and dance

Magnificent trumpets survive from bronze age Ireland. The oldest legends testify to the central position of music in traditional life and the esteem in which musicians, harpists and pipers in particular, were held. Both instruments thrive today, having followed an unbroken succession for thousands of years. Most renowned of the traditional harpists was Turlough O'Carolan who died in 1738.

Dublin in the 18th century became one of the musical capitals of Europe – the venue for the first performance of Handel's "Messiah". The 19th century pianist John Field introduced the nocturne. The opening of the National Concert Hall in 1981 was a major boost to classical music.

The survival of traditional melodies owes much to their use by the poet Thomas Moore (1779-1852) in songs that are still popular today. But Irish music developed by emigrants is also one of the foundations of American Country and Western.

The 20th century has seen world-wide success for Irish groups: some, such as The Chieftains, traditional, others, like U2 and Enya, modern. Music festivals are an outstanding feature of contemporary Irish life as are pubs where musicians perform, even in the smallest villages. In 1994 "Riverdance" dazzled world audiences with new interpretations of traditional Irish steps. Meanwhile such music centres as Ceol, in Dublin's Smithfield, use state-of-the-art electronics to introduce the ancient traditions.

→ The world-renowned Irish group U2.

↑ →→ Festivals and competitions in traditional dance attract many participants, their costume design is inspired by the illumination of the early Christian manuscripts.

Folklore and literature

Winter nights are long in Ireland and the art of the storyteller has been cherished from time immemorial. Although many came to use English - the Brontë sisters were grand-daughters of an Irish raconteur - the oral tradition is associated more with Irish and, latterly, on the western seaboard. Their tales, ranging from great heroic sagas to charming simple stories have been faithfully taken down and the national folklore archive is enormous.

The gradual replacement of Irish by the English language was accompanied by the superb prose, poetry and drama of Swift, Goldsmith and Sheridan among many others.

↑ William Butler Yeats (1865-1939).

← Oscar Wilde (1854-1900).

> *"Come out of charity and dance with me in Ireland."* – W. B. Yeats

The greatest achievements took place around the time of the Gaelic revival of the late 19th century. Many of those who wrote in English relied heavily on the older Celtic traditions. Some, such as Shaw, Joyce and O'Casey left the country to write in exile. Others, including Synge, Yeats and Lady Gregory stayed at home, their crowning contribution being the establishment of the Abbey Theatre.

The award of a Nobel Prize to Seamus Heaney and the critical acclaim awarded to the plays of Brian Friel show that great literature is a thing of the present.

↑ Seamus Heaney (1939).

↙ James Joyce (1882-1941).

Parks, gardens and great houses

Phoenix Park, two and a half square miles of open space in the city of Dublin, was presented to the people of Ireland in 1747. The greatest of all the public parks of Ireland, a space of grass and woodland, playing fields and formal gardens - to say nothing of the Zoo and the residence of the President - it stands as first amongst equals. Every town has its public gardens, while the country is liberally scattered with forest parks and wildlife reserves.

↑ Powerscourt House, Co. Wicklow.

→ Great Sugarloaf Mountain through a window at Powerscourt.

↑ Built by local labour in the 1840s, Birr Castle telescope, Co. Offaly, was the biggest ever made.

↑↑ Mount Stewart House Co. Down.

The landlords in the 18th century built magnificent houses. Their descendants embellished them with gardens. That of Powerscourt, in Co. Wicklow incorporated an entire mountain in its design. The Marquess of Sligo added a fun park and zoo to Westport House. Fota in Co. Cork has a great arboretum and Mount Stewart in Co. Down displays marvellous 20th century garden sculpture. In Co. Laois the 3rd Earl of Rosse laid out a garden and built the greatest telescope in the world.

And that's just five of them. There are so many parks, gardens and stately homes welcoming visitors that it is hard to travel ten miles in any direction without meeting one of them.

← ↑ Westport House, Co. Mayo, a family home since the 17th century and nowadays welcoming visitors who are at liberty to wander through house and gardens.

Sport

Hurling is the name of a thrilling ball game, played with a curved bat of ash called a hurley. The hero Cuchulain as a young lad wielded a bronze hurley – with literally deadly effect on his opponents. Nowadays the players mostly survive to live long and healthy lives. Nevertheless an ancestry of two thousand years is something that few team games can equal.

Of equal antiquity is horse racing. The wonderful green plain known as the Curragh of Kildare has been its centre since the Iron Age. The modern Curragh race course is the venue for the classics and it is surrounded by the top stables in the land. The sport of kings remains immensely popular amongst all social classes.

⇈ Galway Races the greatest of traditional festivals.

The Gaelic Athletic Association promotes hurley and Gaelic football and the great events of the year are the All-Ireland finals, held in Dublin in September. Always popular, Association football rose in esteem following the success in the 1980s and '90s of the national team in coming close to the top in the World Cup.

⤓⤓ Golfing at the Old Head of Kinsale, Co.Cork.

↓ Golflinks at Ashford Castle, near Cong,
Co. Mayo the land of the immortal movie
"The Quiet Man".

There are nearly 400 golf courses in Ireland, all of them in beautiful surroundings, some amidst the finest scenery in the world. Many add a breath of sea air - or even the odd Atlantic gale. Major events include the Smurfit European Open, the Walker Cup and the Murphy's Irish Open. Visitors are warmly welcomed to all, from the simple local links to the most challenging international courses.

A few games, among them tennis, Rugby football and polo, have an element of attachment to particular social classes. But football, racing and hurling are amongst the greatest levellers. People of all degrees of wealth and wisdom join as equals in the observation and dissection of the latest game.

↑ International Financial Services Centre, Dublin.

The Tiger economy

"The Celtic Tiger" sprang into life early in the 1990s, the result of two key factors. Since the 1950s Ireland had been changing from a huge cattle pasture to a nation of high-tech industries and international service centres with a young and brilliant work force. As a poor member of the European Union, huge sums of money were poured in to develop the infrastructure. These two helped to propel the economy into a period of unprecedented growth.

The results include an unparalleled application of paint to houses and an explosion in the numbers of garden centres. The majority of the people, for the first time in centuries, have the money and the leisure to beautify their dwellings. More houses for the expanding population and more cars on the roads marginally reduce the space for gentle living. But this has been accompanied by a new degree of concern for the environment.

Conservation of the open spaces and of historical monuments together with all the other factors which contribute to the quality of life receive more serious attention from the authorities than ever before. The people of Ireland were not beaten by poverty. Their souls will not be destroyed by wealth. Space and time are, happily, still with us.

Adventure

Horse riding

The rich limestone soil of the Irish midlands produces the finest bloodstock and hunters in the world. The rugged peatlands of the west are the home of the Connemara pony, one of the most loveable and hardiest of its kind. Horse riding is enjoyed by all sorts of people, from the super-rich to the children of the poorest of the poor on the outskirts of Dublin. While the Kerrygold Horse Show at the Royal Dublin Society in August is the social summit of the year, scarcely a summer weekend passes without a show or an event in some part of the country. Top competitors come together for the Three-day Event at Punchestown, in beautiful rolling countryside in the month of May.

Forty-five equestrian centres are listed in the official guide - and there are many others. Without exception they are surrounded by beautiful country and many have the seaside as an added bonus. Most of them are residential and have qualified instructors who will do anything from teaching beginners to training the experts.

Trail-riding for a few days or an entire holiday opens a wonderful vista, the joy of the horse and like-minded company and access to scenery known to few. And, at the other end of the scale of exercise, the horse-drawn caravan offers the extreme in leisure: ambling along country roads at peace with the world whose inhabitants wave to you from their cars as they hurry by.

Water sports

Sailing officially became fun in Ireland in 1720. That was when the Cork Yacht Club was founded, the first of its kind in the world. The open coast on the west, exposed to all the fury of the Atlantic Ocean and its winds is a place for thrills for experienced sailors in sturdy craft. To sail around Ireland, meeting anything from calm to gale force is a challenge for the very best.

But most of the harbours of Ireland are situated in well sheltered bays, windy enough for fun and safe enough for small boats and beginners. This is where most of the action takes place. Sailing courses, most of them residential, are available at all levels on every coast and by some of the big lakes.

→ Horse riding – friendship and thrills on a Connemara shore.

The sheltered bays provide conditions which are calm enough for canoeing to be safe, but with enough wind to gladden the heart of any wind-surfer. Access to thousands of remote coves - and hundreds of lakes - is easy for those who prefer uncrowded places. Or there are popular spots, such as Dublin Bay, where the fun lies in having plenty of company. And for those who enjoy exposure to the elements there are fantastic surfing opportunities in the west. County Sligo offers some of the finest.

Subaqua diving and exploration has endless possibilities - and plenty of backup in the form of well established clubs and experienced boatmen. Marine life is abundant, there are many caves and a great number of wrecked ships, including several from the Spanish Armada.

Once something of a menace, the sea around Ireland today is a boundless space for adventure - and it's never more than 100 km from any point in the country.

↖ Traditional sailboats in Connemara, Co. Galway.

← Reared in the rocky moorland of the west coast, the Connemara pony is hardy, gentle, affectionate - and a prince amongst jumpers.

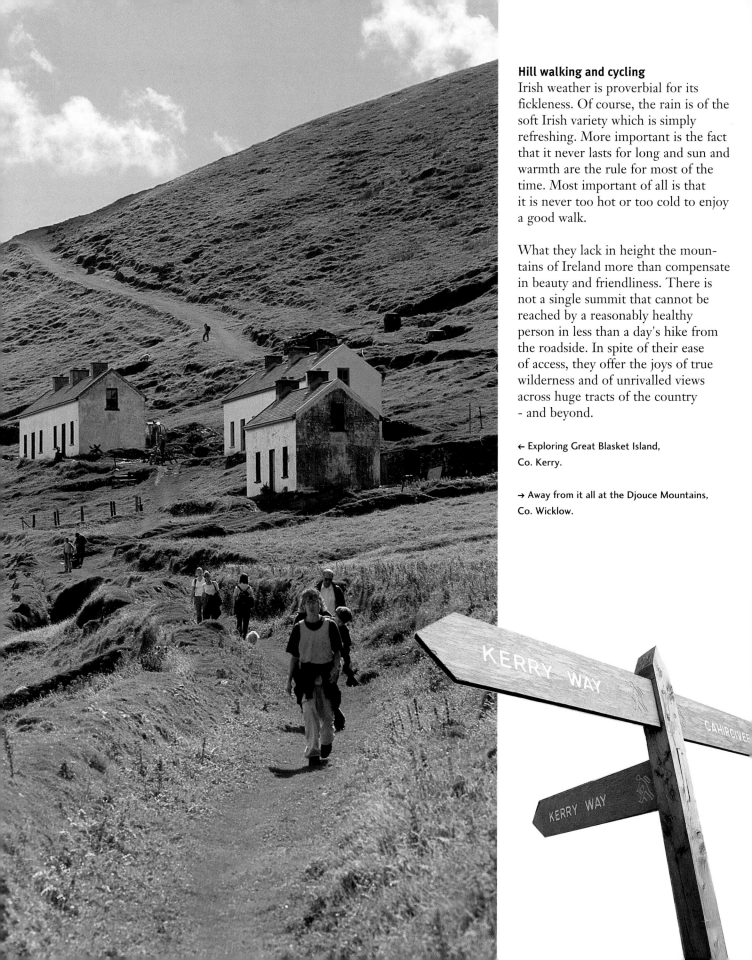

Hill walking and cycling

Irish weather is proverbial for its fickleness. Of course, the rain is of the soft Irish variety which is simply refreshing. More important is the fact that it never lasts for long and sun and warmth are the rule for most of the time. Most important of all is that it is never too hot or too cold to enjoy a good walk.

What they lack in height the mountains of Ireland more than compensate in beauty and friendliness. There is not a single summit that cannot be reached by a reasonably healthy person in less than a day's hike from the roadside. In spite of their ease of access, they offer the joys of true wilderness and of unrivalled views across huge tracts of the country - and beyond.

← Exploring Great Blasket Island, Co. Kerry.

→ Away from it all at the Djouce Mountains, Co. Wicklow.

Most of the mountain ranges now have at least one way-marked trail and a book to describe it. The trails make a handy way to start on a particular region. There are also numerous "hill-walkers' guides" which concentrate on showing the best paths to the most popular peaks. And there are several centres which arrange for guided walks.

Cycling in Ireland is for the fairly energetic traveller. There are many hills which, of course, means downhills too. Three great advantages are the abundance of B and Bs, the frequency of villages, so that any day's route is within easy reach of food and lodging and the infinite network of quiet back-roads. For those who prefer to camp,

few farmers will refuse permission for a wanderer to spend a night on the land.

The tradition of welcoming the stranger is a strong one.

Rock climbing and caves

The choice of cliffs to climb in Ireland is almost unlimited. At one extreme, Dubliners trek to deepest suburbia to scale the heights of Dalkey quarry. Most of this granite hill was removed in the 18th and 19th centuries, leaving an entirely satisfying array of rock faces to entertain all from the most experienced climber to the beginner. For day-trippers from the capital, the Glendalough valley is another favourite.

↑ The welcoming underworld of
Aillwee Cave, Co. Clare.

← Scaling the heights of Dalkey Quarry,
Co. Dublin.

But most of the climbs are in mountain ranges or on sea cliffs which, while far from crowds, are all easily approached by good roads - with the exception of a number of enticing climbs on island cliffs. The limestone escarpments of County Sligo offer some of the best climbing, amongst stupendous scenery. County Donegal includes the challenge of Dunaff Head said to be "unclimbable" together with a host of more welcoming and well-explored cliffs in the Poisoned Glen and Bluestack Mountains.

Limestone is the rock which lies beneath a large proportion of the land of Ireland. And that means a multitude of caves. Ailwee in County Clare is a delight for the visitor: entered through an excellent visitor centre and provided with electric light. A little farther from the tourist trail is Mitchelstown Cave, the finest of all: so much like a cathedral that they even arrange concerts of church music. For the true explorer, the cave systems of Counties Clare and Fermanagh are unending and, in parts, yet unknown.

Fishing

Irish people have been fishing for salmon for ten thousand years - so it is not surprising that to this day it retains an almost mystical appeal. Salmon can be caught in nearly every river, but some, such as the Moy, the Corrib and the Munster Blackwater are particularly good. The other popular native fish is the brown trout, found in lakes and rivers everywhere.

Catering for the visitor, native and foreign, is one of the best traditions in sports fishing. Over many generations, specialist hotels and guest houses have grown up, most of them owned by fishing enthusiasts, and providing boats and ghillies - assistants unrivalled for good company and their knowledge of where the fish lie and how to catch them.

→ Lough Gill, Co. Sligo.

↑ Salmon fishing on the Erriff, Co. Mayo.

The odd term of "coarse fish" is used for freshwater species other than salmon and trout. Lakes, slow-flowing rivers and canals are their haunts and Ireland has a great many of them. The myriad lakes on the River Erne in the north midlands are amongst the most popular and visiting anglers are faced with a bewildering choice both of good fishing grounds and of places to stay. Pike grow to large sizes, 30 pounds and more and lead solitary lives. Roach on the other hand are small and abundant.

Sea fishing offers a marvellous variety both of fish species and of places to catch them. Shore angling, from beach or rock ledge, yields cod and pollack and many others. Small boats and large, sea-going boats for the really intrepid hunter for shark and tuna, are available all around the coast. Some small ports, such as Ballycotton on the south coast, are specialists in catering for visiting sea anglers.

Fishing festivals and competitions take place throughout the year. The Irish Specimen Fish Committee is the official body which maintains a wonderful record of big fish and has an annual award ceremony to present certificates to their captors.

→ The Curragh, sturdy boat for the Atlantic waves, built to a design used for more than a thousand years.

Top ten visitor attractions

1 The National Gallery

2 Dublin Zoo

3 The Book of Kells

4 Guinness Storehouse

5 Hugh Lane Gallery

6 Bunratty Castle & Folk Park

7 Irish Museum of Modern Art

8 Waterford Crystal Visitor Centre

9 St. Patrick's Cathedral

10 Rock of Cashel

Author's favourites

1 Birr Castle

2 Clonmacnoise

3 Craggaunowen

4 Dublin Zoo

5 Fota Island

6 The Giant's Causeway

7 The Japanese Gardens

8 Mount Stewart Gardens

9 Trinity College

10 Westport House

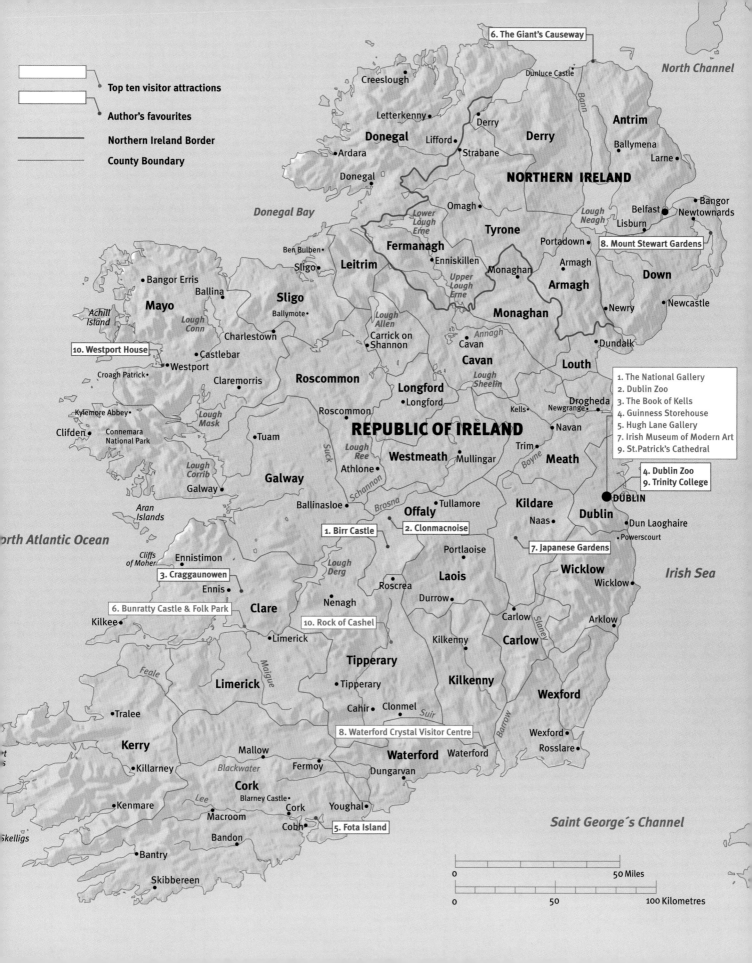

Legend:
- Top ten visitor attractions
- Author's favourites
- Northern Ireland Border
- County Boundary

1. The National Gallery
2. Dublin Zoo
3. The Book of Kells
4. Guinness Storehouse
5. Hugh Lane Gallery
7. Irish Museum of Modern Art
9. St.Patrick's Cathedral

4. Dublin Zoo
9. Trinity College

6. The Giant's Causeway
8. Mount Stewart Gardens
10. Westport House
1. Birr Castle
2. Clonmacnoise
3. Craggaunowen
6. Bunratty Castle & Folk Park
10. Rock of Cashel
7. Japanese Gardens
8. Waterford Crystal Visitor Centre
5. Fota Island

North Channel
Donegal Bay
North Atlantic Ocean
Irish Sea
Saint George's Channel

NORTHERN IRELAND
REPUBLIC OF IRELAND

Creeslough
Letterkenny
Derry
Ballymena
Larne
Donegal
Ardara
Lifford
Strabane
Derry
Antrim
Donegal
Bangor
Newtownards
Belfast
Lisburn
Omagh
Tyrone
Lough Neagh
Fermanagh
Lower Lough Erne
Enniskillen
Monaghan
Armagh
Down
Newcastle
Upper Lough Erne
Ben Bulben
Sligo
Leitrim
Monaghan
Newry
Dundalk
Bangor Erris
Ballina
Sligo
Ballymote
Lough Allen
Cavan
Annagh
Louth
Mayo
Achill Island
Lough Conn
Charlestown
Carrick on Shannon
Cavan
Lough Sheelin
Kells
Drogheda
Newgrange
Castlebar
Westport
Croagh Patrick
Claremorris
Roscommon
Longford
Longford
Navan
Trim
Meath
Mullingar
Kylemore Abbey
Lough Mask
Tuam
Roscommon
Westmeath
Boyne
Clifden
Connemara National Park
Lough Corrib
Suck
Lough Ree
Athlone
Shannon
Brosna
Galway
Galway
Lough Derg
Tullamore
Offaly
Kildare
Naas
Dublin
DUBLIN
Dun Laoghaire
Powerscourt
Aran Islands
Ballinasloe
Portlaoise
Wicklow
Cliffs of Moher
Ennistimon
Laois
Wicklow
Ennis
Roscrea
Durrow
Carlow
Arklow
Kilkee
Nenagh
Kilkenny
Carlow
Slaney
Limerick
Clare
Tipperary
Tipperary
Kilkenny
Wexford
Tralee
Feale
Maigue
Cahir
Clonmel
Suir
Wexford
Rosslare
Kerry
Mallow
Fermoy
Dungarvan
Waterford
Waterford
Killarney
Blackwater
Blarney Castle
Youghal
Kenmare
Lee
Cork
Cobh
Macroom
Bandon
Bantry
Skibbereen

0 ——— 50 Miles
0 ——— 50 ——— 100 Kilometres

About the author

Dr. Christopher Moriarty, scientist and writer, born on 14 March 1936 has been engaged in a love affair with Ireland for more than half a century. His work as a specialist in inland fisheries has kept him travelling to every part of the country and given him a unique opportunity to observe the landscape and people. One of his greatest pleasures is sharing his knowledge of the country with friend and stranger.

A selection of his books:
"The book of Liffey" 1988,
"Down the Dodder" 1991,
"Byways rather than Highways" 1993,
"Exploring Dublin; wildlife, parks, waterways" 1997.
He also contributes regular articles to the Irish Tourist Board's magazine "Ireland of the Welcomes".

About us

We, the Terrascope team, wish to share with you the fascination and concern for our planet. A thrill to discover and a must to preserve.

That is why we created the Terrascope series, a new way of capturing the atmosphere and impressions of your travel destinations. The books are distinctive for their stylish and easily recognisable design, lavishly endowed with photographs and the text is written by local authors with knowledge and passion. This makes the Terrascope series a unique and lasting gift.

Our belief is that exploring the world, equates with caring for the world. Therefore a part of the Terrascope proceeds is set aside for humanitarian and environmental projects, helping people, animal life and Nature.

The Terrascope books are available at your travel destinations. Read more about us on our web site, or write us a letter with comments or travel discoveries you would like to share with us. We look forward to hearing from you.

www.terrascope-books.com

In:Corporate books / Terrascope
Waldemar Thranesgt. 77
NO-0175 Oslo
Norway

Picture credits

Top = A
Top left = B
Top right = C
Bottom = D
Bottom left = E
Bottom right = F
Centre left = G
Centre right = H
Centre = I

Ivan O. Driscoll: 20, 51 H

Mary Evans Picture Library:
84 A, 84 D, 85 D

Image Bank: 30-31, 63, 93 A,

The Irish Tourist Board
/Bord Failte: 16, 19, 23 F, 24 A,
26, 36 I, 39 A, 47 C, 53 C, 61 F,
65 E, 65 F, 86 H, 90 D, 93 D, 98,
99 C, 100 I, 104 A, 106 E

Keewi photography:
15 F, 22, 48 D, 101

Richard T. Mills: 100 H

Nutan: 8

Photo Images: 1, 14, 21, 33 A,
36 B, 48 A, 66 E

Samfoto
/Morten Andersen:
49 D, 67 B, 92 G
/Mimsy Møller: 62, 68
/Malin Gezelius/Mira: 67 C
/Nina Korhonen/Mira:
70 E, F and DI
/Pål Hermansen:
33 H, 72-73, 75 D, 94, 95 B,
106-107

Scanpix: 66 G, 81 D, 85 C, 108

The Board
of Trinity College: 13

The Slidefile : 10-11, 12 A, 12 D,
15 I, 15 C, 17 A, 17 D, 18 B, 18 G,
23 A, 23 E, 24 D, 25 B, 25 F,
25 G, 28-29, 33 F, 34 B, 34 E,
34 H, 35 B, 35 D, 37, 38-39,
39 E, 39 C, 40, 41 A, 41 D,
42-43, 44-45, 46, 47 G, 49 A,
50, 51 H, 52 A, 52 D, 53 G,
54 A, 55, 56 D, 56-57 A, 58,
59 A, 59 D, 60-61, 61 F, 64-65,
66 A, 66 F, 67 D, 69 B, 69 C,
70 A, 71, 75 A, 76 B, 76 C, 77,
78 B, 78 E ,78 H, 79, 80 A,
80 D, 81 A, 82 A, 82 D, 83,
86 B, 87 A, 87 D, 88-89, 89 C,
90 B, 91, 92 C, 95 C, 95 E, 99 F,
102, 103, 104 D, 105, 106 B, 112

Tony Stone:
2-3, 4-5, 6-7, 27, 32, 36 C,
43 C, 74, 96-97

Cover front: Slidefile, Samfoto,
Irish Tourist Board/Bord Failte
Cover back: Tony Stone,
Slidefile

Cover front:
· Symbol of Ireland – Shamrock.
· Rock of Cashel, Co. Tipperary.
· St Patrick Stained Glass from
  Glogheen Church,
  Co. Tipperary.
· Trinity College in Dublin.
· Folkmusic in Pub in Bunbeg.
· Giant's Causeway, Co. Antrim.
· Happy school girls in Dublin.

Cover back:
· The Cliffs of Moher, Co. Clare.
· Waterfront Hall in Belfast.
· Horseback riding in
  Connemara, Co. Galway.